Full of BEANS

Poetry for Children

**Written and Illustrated
by
Jo Hudson**

Copyright 2023

Full of Beans

It's been said I'm full of beans.
They're coming out my ears.
They're rolling off my shoulders.
I cry them in my tears.

I wonder if they're red or brown,
Skinny, long and green,
Lima, wax, or pinto,
Or colored jelly beans?

I plan to catch them as they fall
Or swoop them with a scoop.
And when I finally have enough
I'll make bean soup.

I'll be a famous chef,
Win awards for my cuisine,
And prove there's nothing wrong
With being full of beans.

The Wild Goose Race

Gwendolyn loved to run
And waddle, wiggle, waggle.
She was the fastest goose
Of any local gaggle.

Wild geese everywhere caught wind
Of Gwendolyn's quick pace
And flew in by the flocks
To run the Wild Goose Race.

On GO day when the flag dropped,
Gwen called out, "Its no race!
If you think that you can catch me,
You're on a wild goose chase!"

Teetering Tater Toppings

Under the cheese that's under my chin,
On top of my potato skin,
If I'm not mistaken, are onions and bacon,
Mushrooms and brie, and a broccoli tree.
There are chunks of a carrot, strings of a bean.
There are so many toppings they're starting to lean.
A cherry tomato has rolled off the table.
It's over by the door.
The rest of the toppings are slipping and slopping
And falling on the floor.
When it's all said and done, after all of the rumble,
What's left is a spud, be it ever so humble.

Abby the Happy Crab

Abby is a happy crab.
Hide and seek in the sand.
Turtle tag, side to side.
Peek-a-boo with the tide.
Sandcastle beach parties.
Marco Polo in the sea.
Least crabby at the ocean?
Happy Abby, the crustacean.

Mabelline's Green Thumb

Mabelline found a seed
And thought that it might grow
So she planted it in a little cup,
Gave it a drink of water,
A great big gardener hug,
And watched to see what it might become.

Mabelline's tiny seed
Didn't seem to want to grow.
She wondered if it was just a weed.
Would it ever sprout?
Should she throw it out?
What if it was never meant to be?

Then one day a little leaf
Peeked bravely through the dirt,
Looked around and turned to face the sun.
Mabelline saw the sprout,
And once she saw the stem,
She gave herself two green thumbs up!

Billy the Show Goat

Billy the show goat got dressed to the hilt
In a fancy coat with tails
And climbed up to the mountaintop
To dance for a yak and a quail.

By the start of the show, Billy's belly was bare
So he had to confess to his fans
That he'd eaten his clothes on the way there
And was sorry he didn't have pants.

The quail and the yak were taken aback
And quickly abandoned the place.
So Billy the show goat took a grand bow
And said, "I guess it's a matter of taste!"

Detective McNarf

Waldo McNarf is quite the detective.
He's got an intuitive eye.
He wears a long coat
Lined with all kinds of gadgets
To help him when he spies.

There's a fingerprint lifter, invisible ink,
A pen that records everything that you think.
A notebook for clues, a telescope spier,
A flashlight, some string, and a round magnifier.

Waldo McNarf is quite the detective.
He's got a very famous face.
All he needs now
Is something suspicious
So he can solve the case.

Otter's Goggles

Oscar the otter was afraid of water.
He would only swim on his back.
To avoid a squabble, Oscar wore goggles
When he took his daily bath.

Kite Tale

The tail of my kite is a wonderful thing
Made up of treasures tied to a string.
There's a long striped stocking, a tiny toy car,
A red rubber snake and a green dinosaur,
Three pieces of taffy, a banana, a key,
A pencil, a sailboat, a twig from a tree.
But a kite can't go up, up to the clouds
With a tail that's too heavy to get off the ground.

City Cow

On a busy street corner
In the center of town
The featured attraction
Was Dottie the cow.

People from far
And people from wide
Came to the city
To see such a sight.

They heard Dottie's "Moo!"
They rubbed Dottie's nose,
Until one day the gate
Didn't quite close.

Seeing her chance,
Dottie went for a walk
To visit the flower shop
Right down the block.

FRESH FLOWERS

"HONK! HONK!" went cars.
The florist yelled, "Scat!"
Dottie went home.
She didn't like that.

The next time the gate
Was left just ajar
Dottie the city cow
Stayed in the yard.

Social Butterfly

Rita, the social butterfly, received a personal invitation
To every high-society shindig in the ecosystem.
She hobnobbed with monarchs, tangoed with toucans,
And mingled with anyone who wasn't human.

Garden Adventure

From the tops of cornstalks
Taller than trees,
Spyglass in hand,
I gaze over the seas.

In the distance a ship
Filled with pirates and treasure
Bobs in the waves
In spite of the danger.

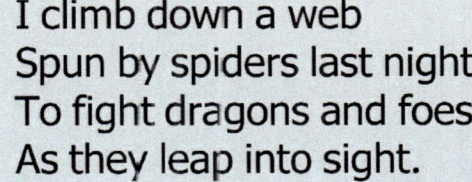

I climb down a web
Spun by spiders last night
To fight dragons and foes
As they leap into sight.

I rescue a scarecrow
Tied to a post,
Jump over a serpent
And scare off a ghost.

A damsel in distress
Cries out from far away,
Calling me for dinner
To come back another day!

Dan D. Lion's Wish

Dan D. Lion had a wish
But didn't know how to make it.
He wanted to be brave
Without having to fake it.

Giraffe told him to wish
Upon a falling star,
But she was tall so, for her,
Stars weren't all that far.

Monkey said that he would
Throw a penny in a pond,
But he had thumbs he could use
To complete the toss.

Elephant wished on candles
When his birthday rolled around.
His trunk made birthday candles
Easy to blow out.

Owl told Dan to make his wish
In his heart and he would see
That there he'd find all the things
He wished that he could be.

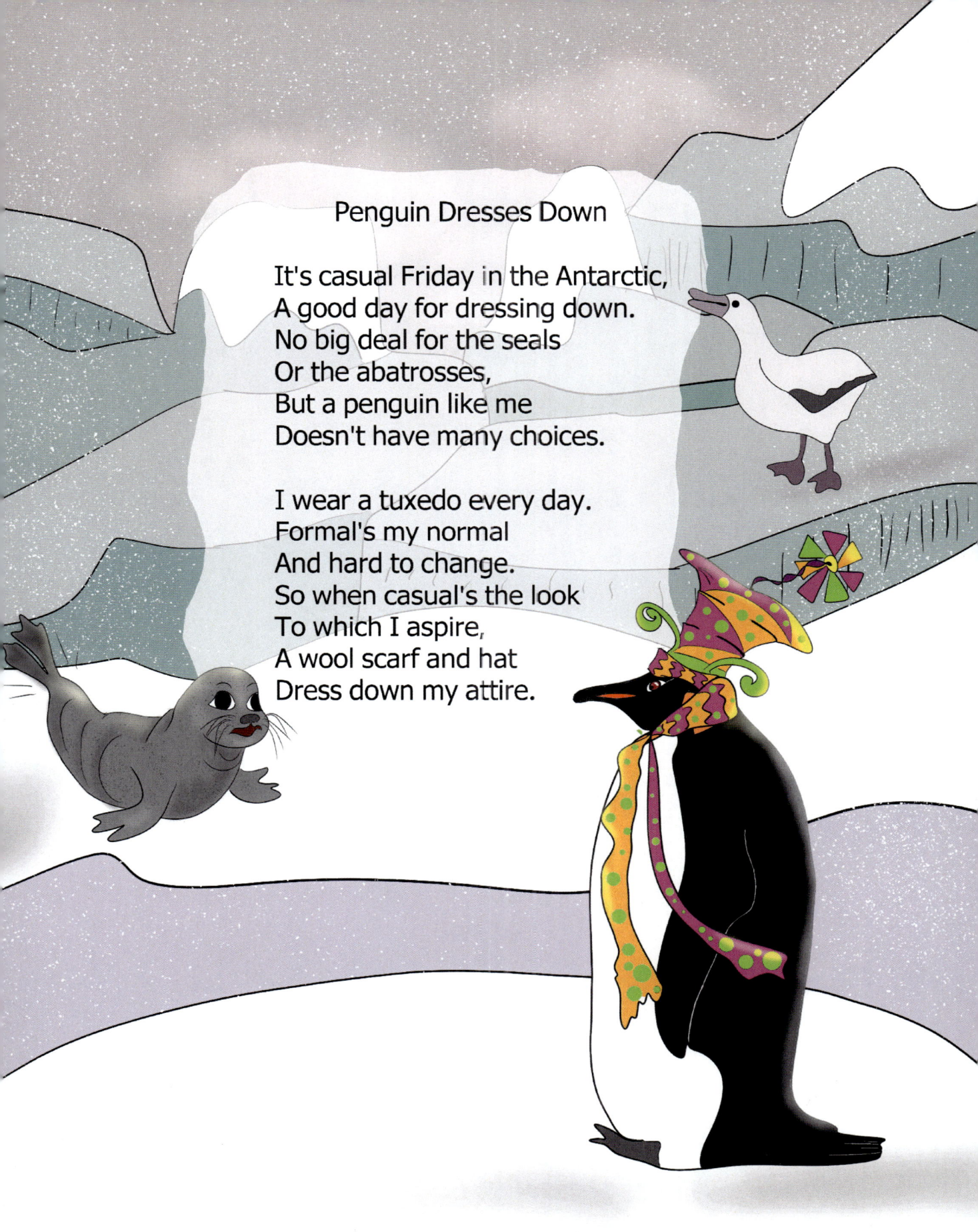

Penguin Dresses Down

It's casual Friday in the Antarctic,
A good day for dressing down.
No big deal for the seals
Or the abatrosses,
But a penguin like me
Doesn't have many choices.

I wear a tuxedo every day.
Formal's my normal
And hard to change.
So when casual's the look
To which I aspire,
A wool scarf and hat
Dress down my attire.

Baby Bird's Parachute

Baby Bird knew it was time
To try out his new wings.
Brother Bird and Sister Bird
Weren't worried about a thing.

Baby Bird made a grand plan
That he would execute
When it came his turn to jump,
He'd use a parachute.

His plan worked like a charm.
He landed safely on the ground.
Trouble was, the other birds
Flew up instead of down.

Pretty Pig

Pinky the pig loved to be clean.
She refused to go into the mud.
She would not wade or wallow.
She'd rather bathe in a tub.

Pinky said she was a "pretty pig."
The other swine were befuddled.
What kind of pig was too snooty
To put even a hoof in a puddle?

Pinky was pretty but lonely.
She wanted to join in the fun.
How could she stay clean and still
Not be such a stick in the mud?

The piglets and sows held a meeting
And the hogs in the sty were hired
To move Pinky's tub of bubbles
Into the muck and the mire.

After that when the pigs would wallow,
Pinky was there center bog,
Squealing and snorting with friends,
Joining in without going whole hog.

Puddle Jumper

Percy B. Fuddle
Jumps puddle to puddle
To get to new locations.

He waits each day
For clouds of gray
And more precipitation.

The Numbers Kid

Nora is a numbers kid.
She plays with numbers in her head,
Dumps them out on the floor,
Takes some away then adds some more.

She stands six and seven next to eight.
It is her favorite numbers game.
Nora's fun is multiplied
When they fall over and divide.

The Creatures of Habit

The creatures of Habit are in a rut.
They do the same thing every day.
Walk the same walk. Talk the same talk.
Replay. Replay. Replay.

When you meet a creature of Habit,
You'll know it by its feet.
They'll be going around in circles.
Repeat. Repeat. Repeat.

The best thing for a creature of Habit,
Once you become its friend,
Is to get it to try something new.
Again and again and again.

THE VERY BIG BOOK

Percy had a favorite book.
It was as big as him.
He'd read it front to back
Then read it once again.

He pulled it in his wagon
He took it everywhere.
When others asked to read it,
Percy wouldn't share.

Which made them think it was
The best story every heard,
When all that was inside
Was one humongous WORD.

VERY BIG BOOK

WO RD

Little Frog's Big Voice

When the Lily Pad Choir conductor
Put out a call for talent,
Little Frog was eager to join in.
On the day of the auditions,
He practiced until dusk.
"RIBBIT. RIBBIT. RIBBIT."

"You're too small," croaked the judges
When Little Frog took center stage.
"You're no bigger than a polliwog!"
But the whole swamp stopped to listen to
"RIBBIT. RIBBIT. RIBBIT."
In the big voice of a little frog.

The Little White Lion

I told a little white lion
That he was a mouse.
Lion's aren't allowed
In my mother's house.

I hid him in a little box
Because he was so small.
It wasn't like he was
A real lion, after all.

"Are you sure I'm a mouse?"
My lion roared one day.
"I'm getting so much bigger
And mice don't sound this way."

As much as I insisted,
Hard though I may have tried,
A lion is a lion
And lion's just can't hide.

Fancy Cat

Fancy lived a life of luxury.
She was a pampered pet.
She lounged all day like royalty
And played with golden thread.

She only snacked on five-star treats.
She'd rather go without.
The silken blanket at her feet
Was the cat's meow.

But Fancy envied other cats
Romping here and there with glee,
And renounced her stately status
To be simply fancy free.

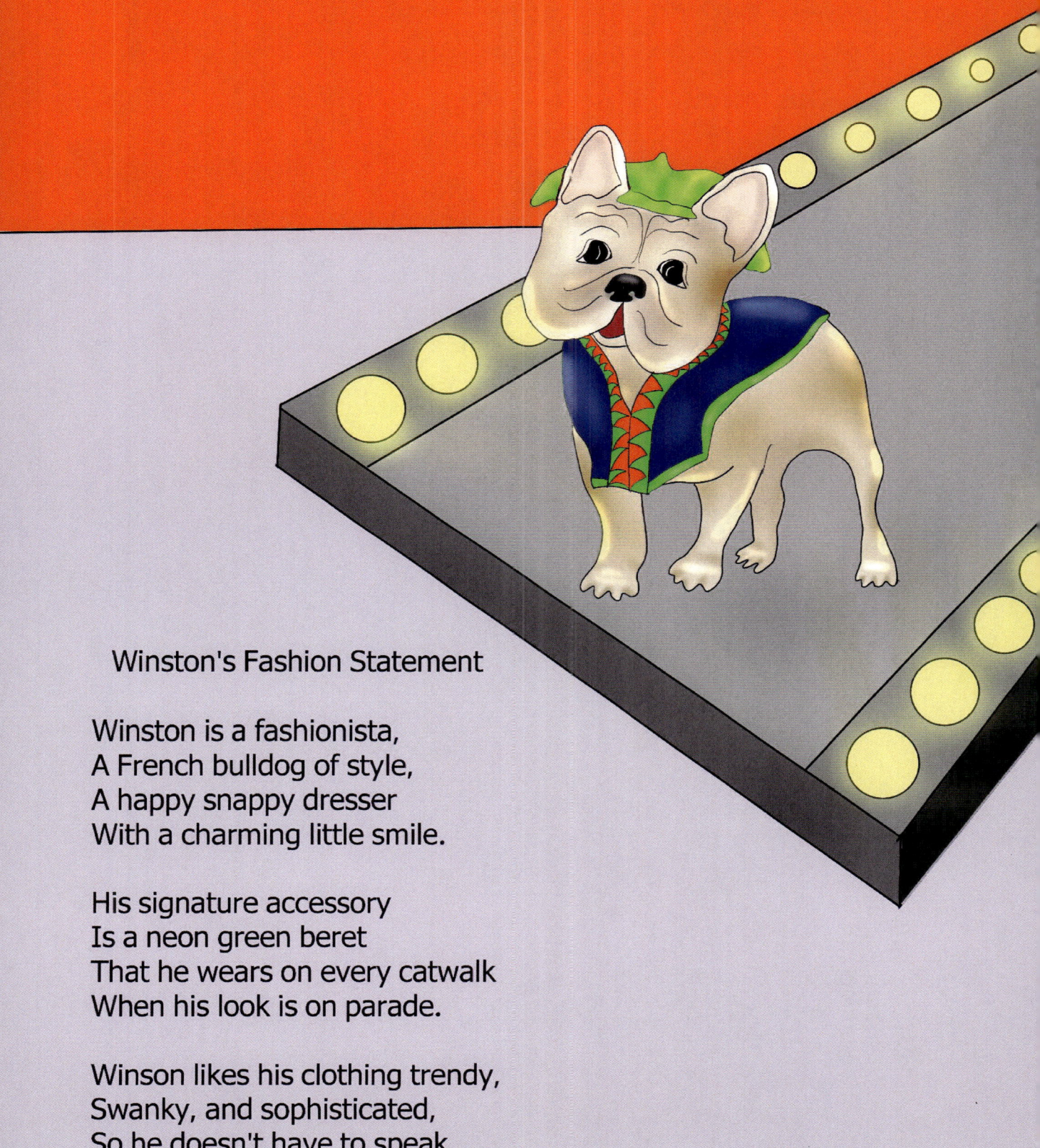

Winston's Fashion Statement

Winston is a fashionista,
A French bulldog of style,
A happy snappy dresser
With a charming little smile.

His signature accessory
Is a neon green beret
That he wears on every catwalk
When his look is on parade.

Winson likes his clothing trendy,
Swanky, and sophisticated,
So he doesn't have to speak
To make his fashion statement.

Odd Sock Out

Odd Sock Out went for a tumble
And clung to the back of a shirt.
It was part of his overall master plan

To make his escape from the sock drawer,
Kick off his old leather shoes,
And travel to far and distant lands.

To the other socks in the bureau
Odd Sock Out was a super hero
And they his tight-knit group of fans.

Hopscotch

Hopscotch the kangaroo jumped higher every day.
From the time his paws touched the ground, he was on his way.

What started out as a hop soon became a leap
And before too long Hopsotch joined the school track team.

At their first offical track meet, the coach took him aside.
The other team thought Hopscotch was overqualified.

Hopscotch glanced across the field and also thought it funny
That the opposing team was of a class of Easter bunnies.

Little Lost Shadow

I lost my shadow again last night.
It was nowhere to be found.
We were together all day long.
It was right there on the ground.

I looked inside my socks and shoes,
Under rocks and under stones,
But shadows know just where to hide.
Where that is nobody knows.

When I went outside this morning,
Sunshine bright upon my face,
My shadow was there waiting
And ready to take its place.

The Whistling Moon

The man in the moon
Whistled a tune
And tickled the clouds in the sky,
Who caught a ride,
Along with the tide,
To a quiet place in the night.

The leaves in the trees
Felt a slight breeze
And rustled a soft lullaby
That sang me to sleep
With a tune that we keep,
The whistling moon and I.

SCAVENGER HUNT

Help Detective McNarf find each of these things somewhere in the pages of this book!

Made in the USA
Las Vegas, NV
11 October 2024